M
MEASURE

NOTES

[in]cluding

- *Introduction to Shakespeare*
- *Introduction to* Measure for Measure
- *Synopsis*
- *List of Characters*
- *Summaries and Commentaries*
- *Character Analyses*
- *Critical Interpretation*
- *Selected Bibliography*

L. Hillegass, M.L.S.
[U]niversity of Denver

INCORPORATED
LINCOLN, NEBRASKA 68501

ISBN 0-8220-0049-0

Printed in U.S.A.

1991 Printing

Cliffs Notes, Inc. Lincoln, Nebraska

CONTENTS

Measure for Measure Notes

INTRODUCTION TO SHAKESPEARE

Two books are essential to the library of any English-speaking household; one of these is the Bible, the other is the works of William Shakespeare. These books form part of the household furnishings, not as reading material generally, but as the symbols of religion and culture – sort of a twentieth-century counterpart of the ancient Roman household gods. This symbolic status has done a great deal of damage both to religion and to Shakespeare.

Whatever Shakespeare may have been, he was not a deity. He was a writer of popular plays, who made a good living, bought a place in the country, and retired at the age of about forty-five to enjoy life as a country gentleman. The difference between Shakespeare and the other popular playwrights of his time was that he wrote better plays – plays that had such strong artistic value that they have been popular ever since. Indeed, even today, if Shakespeare could collect his royalties, he would be among the most prosperous of playwrights.

During the eighteenth century, but mostly in the nineteenth, Shakespeare's works became "immortal classics," and the cult of Shakespeare-worship was inaugurated. The plays were largely removed from their proper place on the stage and were taken into the library where they became works of literature, rather than drama, and were regarded as long poems, attracting all the artistic and pseudo-artistic atmosphere surrounding poetry. In the nineteenth century this attitude was friendly but later, and especially in the early twentieth century, a strange feeling arose in the English-speaking world that poetry was sissy stuff, not for men but for women's clubs. This, of course, is sheer nonsense.

This volume will present a detailed analysis of *Measure for Measure* and background information which will show the play in its proper perspective. This means seeing the play in relation to the other plays, to the history of the times when they were written, and in relation to the theatrical technique required for their successful performance.

G. B. Harrison's book *Introducing Shakespeare*, published by Penguin Books, will be of value for general information about Shakespeare and his plays. For reference material on the Elizabethan theater, consult E. K. Chambers, *The Elizabethan Theatre* (four volumes). For study of the organization and production methods of this theater, see *Henslowe's Diary*, edited by W. W. Greg. For general reading, the student will enjoy Margaret Webster's *Shakespeare without Tears*, published by Whittlesey House (McGraw-Hill) in 1942.

INTRODUCTION to *Measure for Measure*

Measure for Measure is known to have been performed by Shakespeare's company at the Court of James I on December 26, 1604. It is generally presumed to have been written in the same year. The earliest printed text appeared in the First Folio, published in 1623. Confusions and imperfections in that text suggest that errors may have been made in transcription, and further, that the play may have undergone revision at some time prior to its first printing.

The basic plot which Shakespeare employed in *Measure for Measure* was not new to that play. Its ultimate source was a historical incident supposed to have occurred near Milan in 1547. A young wife prostituted herself to save her condemned husband. The magistrate who had forced the woman to yield to him proceeded to execute her husband. He was eventually made to marry the widow and was then put to death himself for his crime against her.

This incident was probably the basis of a story by Giraldi Cinthio, published in 1565 as the eighty-fifth novel in his *Hecatommithi*. The same plot was also put to use in Cinthio's *Epitia*, a dramatic version which appeared in 1583, some ten years after the death of its author. In 1578, after Cinthio's death, but before the publication of his dramatic version, George Whetstone, an English dramatist, wrote his *Promos and Cassandra*, using Cinthio as his source. The play was never performed, but a story based on it was included in 1582, as a tale in Whetstone's *Heptameron of Civill Discourses*.

Shakespeare probably was aware of all four of Cinthio's and Whetstone's versions of the basic plot. He may also have known of the original true incident and of other similar, supposed historic situations on record. However, Shakespeare departed from his sources in several areas. In considering *Measure for Measure*, it is important to be aware of the source versions and the changes Shakespeare made in adapting the plot for his own purposes.

In Cinthio's first version, Epitia is the sister of a young man condemned to death for the crime of rape. Juriste promises to pardon him if she will submit her body to him. She does, but Juriste has her brother executed anyway and cruelly sends her the body. She appeals to the Emperor, who forces Juriste to marry her and then condemns him to death. Epitia begs for his life, and he is pardoned.

In Cinthio's later drama, a surprise ending is added. The Captain of Justice comes forward in the last act to inform Epitia that he spared her brother's life, sending her a substitute body. Having formerly refused to plead for her husband, she now begs for and is granted his pardon.

In Whetstone's version, the heroine is Cassandra, whose brother Andrugio is condemned to death for seduction rather than rape. She sacrifices her virginity to the demands of Promos, who breaks his promise of pardon for Andrugio, sending her his head. Cassandra takes her case to the King, who forces Promos to marry her and then condemns him to death. It is now learned that the jailer has spared Andrugio, substituting the head of another. When her brother is restored to her, Cassandra pleads for Promos's life which the King spares.

In Shakespeare's *Measure for Measure*, Isabella's brother Claudio is condemned for getting his beloved with child. Isabella begs Angelo for his life, and he promises to spare her brother if she will yield to his desires. She refuses, but through the machinations of the disguised Duke, Mariana takes her place in Angelo's bed. Convinced that he has lain with Isabella, he nevertheless orders the execution of her brother and asks that the head be sent to him as evidence. The Duke persuades the Provost to save Claudio, substituting the head of another. In the final scene, Angelo is made to marry Mariana and is condemned to death. Isabella begs for his life and her prayer is granted by the Duke. She then learns that her brother still lives.

The Shakespearean version of the story is different from the sources in several significant ways. It is a milder handling. For example, Angelo views the supposed head of Claudio himself, while his counterparts in Cinthio and Whetstone send the evidence of execution to the sister. Isabella pleads for Angelo before she learns her brother has been saved, while in Whetstone and in Cinthio's second version, the heroine only begs mercy for the magistrate upon learning of her brother's safety. Escalus is invented by Shakespeare to offer a dramatic contrast to Angelo. The humorous minor characters and the secondary action of which they are a part are Shakespeare's own.

But there are three major ways in which Shakespeare's version is at variance with the sources. First, the Duke plays a major role in *Measure for Measure,* while his counterparts in the sources are merely introduced at the last minute to provide a solution to the conflict at hand. The Duke's disguise, his manipulations of the other characters, and his proposed marriage to Isabella are all new in the Shakespearean version. Second, Isabella refuses to sacrifice her virginity to Angelo. She places her virtue above her brother's life. Her action presents a marked contrast to the background of moral corruption against which it occurs. As a result, the whole business of the substitute bed partner and the character of Mariana are introduced. And third, Shakespeare's heroine does not marry her tormentor. Isabella's virtue is paired in the final scene with the Duke's goodness, rather than with Angelo's vice.

SYNOPSIS

The Duke, Vincentio, deputizing Angelo to act in his place, leaves Vienna, purportedly to make a journey, but in fact to disguise himself as a friar and return to Vienna to watch events transpire. Moral corruption is general in the city where the Duke has been lax in enforcing laws governing such matters. Angelo, eager to make the hand of justice felt, arrests Claudio, a young gentleman who has gotten his beloved Juliet with child. He sentences him to death, although Escalus, an aged advisor of the Duke, urges leniency.

Lucio, a man who keeps company with pimps, bawds, and whores, learns of Claudio's plight from Mistress Overdone, whose whorehouse also falls to Angelo's zeal. Lucio informs Claudio's sister Isabella of his arrest. A religious novice on the verge of entering the sisterhood, she pleads with Angelo to spare her brother.

Angelo is at first adamant, but finding himself tempted by Isabella's beauty, and by her very purity, he offers to pardon Claudio if she will yield her body to him. Isabella refuses, and tells her brother that he must prepare himself for death. When he pleads with her to meet Angelo's demands, she is outraged.

The Duke, disguised as a friar, now takes control of the action. Having reassured Claudio by bringing him to a sense of peace in death, he presents Isabella with a plan which will save both her virtue and her brother's life. Mariana, betrothed to Angelo and forsaken by him, will take Isabella's place in his bed. Isabella agrees and Mariana is met and gives her consent as well. The sexual encounter between Mariana and Angelo takes place in darkness and silence. Although unaware of the substitution, Angelo (in violation of his agreement with Isabella) orders that Claudio's execution proceed. The Duke learns of his intention and arranges to have the head of another prisoner sent to Angelo in place of Claudio's.

Comic action is provided by the play's ribald minor characters, one of whom (Pompey) is made assistant to the executioner, Abhorson. Lucio's gossip about the Duke, related unwittingly to the Duke himself, is another source of humor.

A final confrontation between Isabella and Angelo is staged by the Duke, and Isabella accuses Angelo of his crime, which he denies. The truth is exposed after some suspense in which the Duke (returned to his true identity) pretends to believe Angelo instead of Isabella. The Duke orders Angelo to wed Mariana and then sentences him to death. Begged by Mariana to plead for his life, Isabella at last consents. Angelo is pardoned by the Duke, who now reveals that Claudio is still alive. Having ordered marriages between Claudio and Juliet, and Lucio and his whore, the Duke himself proposes marriage to Isabella.

LIST OF CHARACTERS

Vincentio, the Duke.
Angelo, the Deputy.
Escalus, an ancient Lord.
Claudio, a young gentleman.
Lucio, a fantastic.
Two other gentlemen.

Provost.
Thomas } two friars
Peter }
A Justice.
Varrius.
Elbow, a simple constable.
Froth, a foolish gentleman.
Pompey, a clown; servant to Mistress Overdone.
Abhorson, an executioner.
Barnardine, a dissolute prisoner.
Isabella, sister to Claudio.
Mariana, betrothed to Angelo.
Juliet, beloved of Claudio.
Francisca, a nun.
Mistress Overdone, a bawd.
Lords, Officers, Citizens, a Boy, and Attendants.

SUMMARIES AND COMMENTARIES

ACT I, SCENE i

Summary

The Duke of Vienna meets with his aged advisor, Escalus, to discuss his own imminent departure and a commission which he has for Escalus. The Duke's appointment of Angelo to take his place is mentioned, Escalus agreeing that Angelo is worthy of the honor. The latter arrives and is appointed to rule Vienna in the Duke's absence, in spite of his own suggestion that he be further tested before being so honored.

The Duke declines the offers of Angelo and Escalus to escort him part of the way on his journey. Commenting on his distaste for crowds, he departs. Escalus and Angelo leave together to discuss their respective duties in the Duke's absence, and the scene closes.

Commentary

Three characters are introduced, including two of the three major ones: the Duke and Angelo. The scene establishes the structure within which the action of the play will go forward. A wise monarch is leaving the city in the charge of a younger, less experienced man who is known for his virtue and worth but who, by his own account, is untested.

Escalus, an elderly Lord, stands high in the esteem of his Duke. The nature of the commission which he is given to carry out in the Duke's absence is unclear, due apparently to a missing bit of text in the Duke's first speech.

Angelo is highly praised by both the Duke and Escalus. This praise and the man's own modest reluctance to take over the city's highest post, combine to portray Angelo as a virtuous and capable man who will work for the good of the people. In a frequently quoted speech (I.i.30-41), the Duke compares him to a torch which is lighted not for itself but for the light it can give to those around it.

The Duke is characterized by his own speeches as a man of intelligence and sensitivity who has the good of his people at heart. He announces that he will leave privately: "I love the people, / But do not like to stage me to their eyes" (I.i.68-69). This speech (I.i.68-73), expressing a respect for the people, but a dislike for mob attention, was probably added for the benefit of King James, at whose court the play was first performed. James was well-known for his dislike of a throng.

In deputizing Angelo, the Duke tells him that he has the scope to "enforce or qualify the laws/ As to your soul seems good" (I.i.66-67). That the deputy has the authority to qualify or modify the law and does not exercise it is one of the sources of the play's tragedy.

ACT I, SCENE ii

Summary

Lucio and two other young gentlemen, lounging in the street, exchange wisecracks in a vulgar tone. Mistress Overdone, a whorehouse keeper known to the three, approaches and tells them of the fate of a mutual acquaintance. Young Claudio, arrested for getting Juliet with child, is to be executed some three days hence, at the command of the new deputy, Angelo. Lucio and the others leave to "learn the truth of it" (I.ii.82).

Claudio now comes on stage, guarded by the Provost and his officers. Juliet is also listed in the stage directions as entering at this point. Lucio and his companions return to question Claudio about his arrest. Through Lucio, Claudio sends for his sister Isabella, who is on the point of entering a convent. It is the young man's hope that she will be able to persuade Angelo to be lenient.

Commentary

The reader learns that Angelo will be a stern deputy. In the Duke's absence he has revived laws governing sexual morality which have gone unenforced for nineteen years, by Claudio's count. Not only are all whorehouses surrounding the city to be destroyed, but Claudio, having gotten Juliet with child, is to suffer the full measure of the law.

Claudio, introduced here, speaks with sensitivity and wisdom of his imprisonment, causing Lucio to quip that he "had as lief have the foppery of freedom as the morality of imprisonment" (I.ii.137-39). Claudio is also eloquent in his description of his sister. Altogether, the impression he leaves is that of a calm, intelligent young man.

Although Juliet is mentioned in the stage directions as entering with Claudio, the subsequent dialogue makes her presence seem unlikely. It would be odd of Claudio to speak so openly before her of his crime. Further, in discussing the matter with Lucio, he speaks of Juliet as if she were not present:

> Thus stands it with me: upon a true contract
> I got possession of Julietta's bed:
> You know the lady; she is fast my wife,
> Save that we do the denunciation lack
> Of outward order."
>
> (I.ii.149-53)

Possibly the inclusion of Juliet in the stage directions is an error, or she may have had some part in the scene in an earlier version.

The action of the play takes place on two levels. The main plot unfolds in the polite world, while a parallel minor action occurs among the vulgar characters of the play. This scene introduces the reader to two of the low characters, Mistress Overdone and Pompey. Claudio is another character of the main action, on a level with Angelo, the Duke, and Escalus. Lucio serves as a sort of go-between, a gentleman born to the polite world, whose life style and activities have led him into an acquaintance with the vulgar. Pompey and Mistress Overdone, as well as the "two Gentlemen," speak entirely in prose, while Claudio's lines are delivered exclusively in poetry. Lucio alternates between prose and poetry, depending upon the seriousness of his tone and the persons with whom he is speaking. Shakespeare sets off the two levels of action by this distinction of poetry from prose.

The action of the low plot parallels that of the main. The characters of both are suffering from Angelo's sudden enforcement of the city's morality laws. Claudio is to lose his life, Mistress Overdone her livelihood. The subplot also offers humor to provide a contrast to, and relief from, the tragic vein of the main plot. Lucio, the two Gentlemen, Mistress Overdone, and Pompey exchange witticisms loaded with puns and word plays in the true Shakespearean style.

The repetition of the story of Claudio's arrest and the failure of Mistress Overdone and Lucio to acknowledge it, although they are clearly aware of it, indicates that some revision may have taken place, confusing the issue. It is also possible, however, that Shakespeare used this posture of ignorance to allow for additional witticisms on sex.

ACT I, SCENE iii

Summary

The Duke, seeking refuge at a monastery, explains his purpose to Friar Thomas. Having led Angelo and his people to think he has gone to Poland, he now wishes to disguise himself as a friar in order to go unrecognized among his subjects. He has allowed the "strict statutes and most biting laws,/ The needful bits and curbs to headstrong weeds" (I.iii.19-20) to go unenforced over a period of several years. The laws have been openly flaunted and must now be brought to bear. When the friar gently suggests that it is for the Duke himself, rather than his deputy, to do so, the Duke agrees. However, since the fault is his for allowing the people too much scope, he feels it would seem "too dreadful" (I.iii.34) in him to turn suddenly strict. For this reason he has deputized Angelo. He now wishes to observe his deputy's rule. As the scene closes, the Duke implies that, having reason to doubt Angelo's character, he has made this a sort of test.

Commentary

The Duke's character is further delineated by an admission o his failure to provide discipline for his people. The liberties describe have apparently been allowed because of his love for "the life re moved" (I.iii.8). His preference for a withdrawn life has allowed th abuses to go on over a length of fourteen years (I.iii.21), by th Duke's account, although Claudio, in the previous scene, makes i nineteen years (I.ii.172).

The Duke expresses here the belief that too much liberty mus lead to restraint. He has given the people too wide a scope and mus now strictly enforce the laws to bring his city back under control This is a recurrent theme of the play.

The closing lines of the scene are worthy of note as indicating a suspicion on the part of the Duke that Angelo is not as virtuous as he appears to be:

> Lord Angelo is precise;
> Stands at a guard with envy, scarce confesses
> That his blood flows, or that his appetite
> Is more to bread than stone; hence shall we see,
> If power change purpose, what our seemers be.
> (I.iii.50-54)

Here is evidence for those who view the deputy as a hypocrite rather than an honest man fallen once from virtue.

ACT I, SCENE iv

Summary

In a convent of the sisterhood of Saint Clare, Isabella is about to take her vows. She is interrupted in a conversation with Siste Francisca by a man's voice outside. The nun leaves Isabella to open the door to Lucio who has come to tell her of Claudio's plight. Although at first she doubts her ability to sway Angelo's judgement Lucio convinces her to go to him and plead for mercy.

Commentary

Introduced to Isabella, the audience finds her in conversation with a nun, desiring that upon entry into the convent, she should be subject to stricter restraints. Her religious devotion makes the privileges of the sisterhood seem too liberal.

Lucio greets her in a somewhat jocular tone, but becomes sober upon learning that she is the Isabella he is seeking:

I would not—though 'tis my familiar sin
With maids to seem the lapwing and to jest,
Tongue far from heart—play with all virgins so:
I hold you as a thing ensky'd and sainted,
By your renouncement an immortal spirit,
And to be talk'd with in sincerity,
As with a saint.

(I.iv.31-37)

He speaks to her throughout in a respectful tone, using poetry, not prose. Isabella is a devout woman, capable of inspiring respect even in Lucio, who before and after this scene shows himself a thoroughly disrespectful man with more wit than virtue.

ACT II, SCENE i

Summary

Escalus attempts to convince Angelo that he should treat Claudio's case with mercy, but Angelo remains adamant. Calling in the Provost, he orders him to see to Claudio's execution early the following morning.

At this point, Elbow, a constable, enters with the pimp Pompey, and Froth, a gentleman bawd. Elbow accuses the two of some villainy. They respond to Escalus's questioning with an account of their activities so tedious and nonsensical that Angelo withdraws in disgust, leaving Escalus to judge the affair. The elder statesman at last excuses Pompey and Froth with a warning, and upon learning that Elbow has served in his office over seven years, determines to appoint a new constable in the ward.

Commentary

Escalus's role as a foil to Angelo is evident in the first few lines of this scene. The elder pleads the cause of mercy, while the deputy remains unmoved. Angelo is determined to make an example of Claudio by applying the letter of the law which has so long been disregarded.

Ironic foreshadowing pervades this opening conversation. Escalus asks Angelo to consider that had time and place ever been right, he might himself have been guilty of the crime of which Claudio stands accused. Angelo, however, argues that to contemplate a crime is one thing and to commit it another: "'Tis one thing to be tempted, Escalus,/ Another thing to fall" (II.i.17-18). Angelo tells Escalus not to argue mercy for the criminal, but rather to challenge him to demand the same punishment for himself should he be guilty of the same offense. The law should show no mercy, but treat each one the same. "Let mine own judgement pattern out my death" (II.i.30). Ironically, Angelo does commit (or attempt to commit) the same crime later in the play, and does, in fact, ask that the full measure of the law be dealt him.

The entry of Elbow, Froth, and Pompey provides comic relief to the grave discussion which opens the scene. The conversation of Elbow, the constable, is laden with malapropisms. He uses "benefactors" when he means "malefactors," declares that he "detests his wife before Heaven" when he means "protests," and calls a house of ill-repute "respected" ("suspected").

Accused of some crime against the constable's wife, Froth and Pompey carry on at length, describing the circumstances in such detail that Angelo wearies and leaves the matter to Escalus. At last, in despair of ever getting to the bottom of it, Escalus advises that Elbow allow Pompey to continue in his trade until his crime can be more certainly discovered. Warned to stay away from bawds, Froth exits. Pompey engages in a debate with Escalus on the subject of legislated morality. He concludes that sex is a markedly general crime: "If you head and hang all that offend that way but for ten year together, you'll be glad to give out a commission for more heads" (II.i.251-53). Pompey is threatened with a whipping, but he too escapes with no more than a warning.

The interlude is a humorous one, portraying rich characters with human foibles. Pompey is a frank bawd, matter-of-fact about lust and his willingness to exploit it. Elbow's earnest righteousness and his murder of the English language are equally endearing. And Froth joins in a dialogue with Pompey that smacks heavily of vaudeville.

After Elbow departs, the scene returns to the melancholy topic of Claudio's execution. Shakespeare has Escalus invite a justice to dine with him, apparently for the purpose of closing the scene with a dramatic reference to the impossibility of swaying Angelo from his determination to apply the law literally.

Escalus's light treatment of the vulgar bawds who flaunt Vienna's morality laws presents a strong contrast in this scene to Angelo's relentless punishment of Claudio's similar crime. Escalus's response to the situation seems the more reasonable one. As Pompey comments, only gelding all of Vienna's youth will keep them from their bawdy activities.

ACT II, SCENE ii

Summary

The Provost comes to Angelo to verify his order for Claudio's execution on the following morning. Angelo angrily reiterates the command.

Accompanied by Lucio, Isabella arrives to beg the deputy to reconsider her brother's sentence. Angelo stands firm, but finally suggests that Isabella return on the following day. After her departure, his closing soliloquy reveals that he has been shaken by the temptation her maidenhood represents.

Commentary

In his great reluctance to execute Claudio, the Provost dares to ask Angelo whether he may have reconsidered the sentence. In a brief soliloquy spoken before he is conducted into the deputy's presence, he echoes Pompey's sentiments: "All sects, all ages smack of this vice; and he/ To die for't!" (II.ii.5-6). Angelo, however, is unmoved and chides the Provost for his impertinence.

Isabella arrives with Lucio to plead with Angelo on her brother's behalf. The Provost, still present in the room, wishes her good fortune in asides spoken to himself, while Lucio backs her up as a sort of one-man cheering section. He criticizes her cool approach and urges her to show more fire.

In Isabella's arguments on her brother's behalf and Angelo's response to them, the reader again finds a foreshadowing of the deputy's fall from virtue and the events of the final scene. Isabella suggests that had Angelo been guilty of Claudio's crime, the latter would have been capable of mercy. Commanded to be gone, she is moved to an outburst:

> I would to heaven I had your potency,
> And you were Isabel! should it then be thus?

No; I would tell what 'twere to be a judge,
And what a prisoner.

(II.ii.67-70)

Unwittingly, she exactly describes the order of things to come, for, Angelo, having committed Claudio's act, is at the mercy of his young sister. And she, true to her statement here, saves his life by her merciful intervention.

In lines 72 through 79, Isabella makes direct reference to Christian forgiveness. Christ, she declares, who was in a position to judge us all, showed mercy: Angelo should do likewise. The allusion to the Sermon on the Mount is clear: "Judge not, that ye be not judged. For with what measure ye mete, it shall be measured to you again" (Mark 4.24). But it is the law, according to the deputy, which condemns Claudio.

Isabella now turns to the aspect of the case mentioned earlier in this same scene by the Provost: "Who is it that hath died for this offence?/ There's many have committed it" (II.ii.88-89). Still, Angelo is determined to enforce the law which he says has been long asleep.

Isabella's grief drives her to fine tragic poetry. She compares Angelo to a tyrannous giant. "Man, proud man,/ Drest in a little brief authority" (II.ii.117-18) is too proud of his power to show mercy.

Again the foreshadowing surfaces. Isabella asks Angelo to consider whether he has not some guilt similar to her brother's. Here begins Angelo's temptation, in a series of remarks by Isabella which are subject to dual interpretation. Urged to consider his own lusts, Angelo first considers Isabella as a woman. In an aside, he confesses that his senses are stirred. Immediately, she suggests that she will bribe him, and he no doubt leaps to the conclusion that she is offering him her body, although she goes on to say that her prayers for him will serve as bribery. She offers him predawn "prayers . . . / From fasting maids whose minds are dedicate/ To nothing temporal" (II.ii.153-55), presenting the image of pure, maidenly bodies striking pleading attitudes in the darkness. At this point, he abruptly dismisses her, telling her to wait upon him tomorrow.

In the soliloquy which closes the scene, Angelo is amazed at the stirring of his own lust, admitting that it is Isabella's very purity which tempts him from virtue: "What is't I dream on?/ O cunning enemy, that, to catch a saint,/ With saints dost bait thy hook!" (II.ii.179-81).

This scene juxtaposes mercy with strict interpretation of the law. On the side of mercy stand the Provost, Isabella, and, in the background, Lucio, while Angelo stands for the letter of the law.

The scene is one of major importance to the play, since the passages of eloquent tragic poetry spoken by Isabella rank with those found in the great tragedies of this period. Mercy here comes to the fore as the play's major theme. Isabella achieves the nobility of character which has been attributed to her by her brother and Lucio. Angelo stands firm for the law, and the coming triumph of mercy is seen in the dramatic foreshadowing of his fall.

ACT II, SCENE iii

Summary

The Duke, in his role as a friar, comes to the Provost in the prison to offer his services to the prisoners there. Juliet enters, and the Duke plays his role by questioning her repentance of the sin she has committed with Claudio. He then promises to go to Claudio "with instruction" before his execution.

Commentary

This very brief scene provides the Duke with entrance to the prison and an opportunity to see Claudio, which he needs in order to intervene in the affair.

ACT II, SCENE iv

Summary

The scene opens with a soliloquy by Angelo on the subject of his inability to pray sincerely while tempted by Isabella's appeal. That lady then arrives to ask whether he has relented toward her brother. Angelo tells her subtly that Claudio must die unless she will yield her body to him. She fails to understand and Angelo speaks plainly. Isabella refuses, threatening to expose Angelo, who says he will deny her charges. Isabella leaves to tell Claudio he must prepare himself for his execution.

Commentary

Angelo's opening soliloquy recalls that of King Claudius in *Hamlet*. His attempts to pray are frustrated by his fascination with Isabella. Struggling with his conscience, he finds that his moral gravity has grown tedious and he longs to surrender to his lust, which has been aroused by Isabella's purity. Some critics see Angelo as a thoroughly evil hypocrite who merely masquerades as the moral and staid servant of the state. His moral struggle, portrayed in the opening lines of this scene, seems to deny this interpretation. Another apparent reference to King James's dislike of crowds is found in lines 27-30, when Angelo compares the blood rushing to his heart with the "obsequious fondness" (II.iv.28) of a crowd mobbing its monarch.

Announced by a servant, Isabella arrives to ask Angelo's decision with regard to her brother. Angelo at first states that he must die, then hints subtly that he may yet be saved. His hints become broad, but still Isabella fails to take his meaning. Finally, the deputy asks what Isabella would do if by surrendering her body she might save her brother. In her response, the reader sees again the fine tragic poetry which Shakespeare gave Isabella in the earlier scene between herself and the deputy: "As much for my poor brother as myself:/ That is, were I under the terms of death,/ The impression of keen whips I'ld wear as rubies" (II.iv.99-101).

Asked by Angelo why she earlier condoned her brother's offense and now speaks vehemently against Angelo's like intent, she points out that she would excuse the act of her brother because of her love for him. And again she touches on the theme of the universality of the crime. He is not, she points out, without fellows in his lapse. Claudio suggests that women too are liable to succumb to their desires and plainly offers Isabella her brother's life in exchange for her body. He demands her answer upon the following day and exits.

Isabella is trapped. She cannot accuse him openly, since his reputation would back up his denial. She has no choice but to go to her brother with the story so that he may prepare himself for his execution.

It is important in interpreting Isabella's refusal of Angelo's offer to note her reason for it. "Better it were a brother died at once,/ Than that a sister, by redeeming him,/ Should die for ever" (II.iv.106-8). The reader should remember that Isabella, deeply religious, is on the verge of entering the convent. To her, life is a mere prelude to eternity. In considering Claudio's demands, she is not weighing her brother's life against her virginity, but Claudio's life on earth against the everlasting life of her immortal soul. Further, to submit to Angelo's demands would constitute a sin against God, to whom she is ready to devote her life. Her decision may seem a harsh one from Claudio's standpoint, but by her stern religious values it is logical and right. Isabella firmly believes that her brother will agree with her estimation of the situation.

ACT III, SCENE i

Summary

In the prison, the Duke, disguised as a friar, attempts to comfort Claudio and prepare him for his death with assurances of the ephemerality of life. The Duke exits when Isabella arrives on the scene to tell Claudio of Angelo's treachery and her inability to save him. When he begs her to meet Angelo's demands, Isabella upbraids him and leaves in anger.

The Duke, having eavesdropped on their conversation, returns to tell the prisoner that Angelo's offer was no more than a test; the execution is inevitable. The Duke then goes apart with Isabella to suggest a plan which he declares will save Claudio and be of some help to Mariana. The latter, betrothed to Angelo, was deserted by him when her dowry was lost in a shipwreck. Mariana, if she consents, will be a substitute for Isabella in meeting Angelo's demands. Isabella agrees to the plan.

Commentary

The Duke makes his disguise believable by acting the role he has adopted. As a friar, he makes a lengthy speech (lines 6-41) reminding Claudio of life's little worth. Claudio is comforted and ready to accept his fate when his sister arrives.

The Duke having retired, Isabella informs Claudio that she is unable to stop his execution. She hints that there is a way but one which is impossible to take. Grasping at straws, Claudio questions her. Isabella's explanation is slow and tantalizing, creating a build-up of suspense until she at last reveals Angelo's demands. Claudio's initial response is firm: "Thou shalt not do't" (III.i.103). But the desperation he was brought to by Isabella's slow rendering of her tale begins to take effect, and he slips a bit. Perhaps it would not be a deadly sin. Angelo would surely know. Driven by a fear of death which he describes eloquently in a speech reminiscent from *Hamlet*, he at last begs her to yield to Angelo.

Isabella's response at this point is a show of violent temper, sparing Claudio no accusation. When earlier in the same scene he had shown his readiness to accept his execution, she had proclaimed proudly, "There spake my brother; there my father's grave/ Did utter forth a voice" (III.i.86-87). Now she turns the praise to accusation: "Heaven shield my mother play'd my father fair!/ For such a warped slip of wilderness/ Ne'er issued from his blood" (III.i.141-43). Isabella's critics point to this speech as showing a lack of understanding and compassion. Her defenders, however, point out that Isabella's anger is a defense against her own temptation to yield to a beloved brother's pleas. The outburst both reflects the strained condition of her nerves and awakens Claudio from his self-pity. The reader should remember too that, to Isabella, her brother is asking her to sell her soul, and his too, in exchange for "six or seven winters" (III.i.76) added to his life.

The Duke returns to bring Claudio back to his earlier acceptance of the inevitability of his doom. Claudio repents: "Let me ask my sister pardon. I am so out of love with life that I will sue to be rid of it" (III.i.174-75). He recognizes the rightness of Isabella's decision. Isabella's critics suggest that she should have replied to Claudio's anguished words, but she has gone aside, perhaps out of hearing. Much has been made of the fact that she does not speak to him when he is revealed to be alive in the final scene. However, an impassioned embrace might tell all. Certainly here is an example of the extent to which the play is subject to divergent interpretations. A director might portray Isabella as cold and heartless or as a devoted sister, simply by varying her actions in the two scenes.

When the Duke now takes Isabella aside, his warm praise of her goodness to some extent foreshadows his proposal of marriage in the final scene.

The Duke expresses surprise at Angelo's treachery (III.i.189-90), but a few lines later makes it plain that he is well aware of the man's questionable treatment of his betrothed (III.i.233-39). This conflict is an example of the inconsistencies in the play.

In answer to the Duke's suggestion that there may yet be a way to save Claudio, Isabella declares her willingness to do anything that is not foul.

The bed trick upon which the plot turns is presented. Mariana is characterized as "a poor gentlewoman" (III.i.227), whom Isabella recalls having heard of: "good words went with her name" (III.i.219-20). The Duke stresses the good that will come of the substitution: "the doubleness of the benefit defends the deceit from reproof" (III.i.266-68). Isabella will not only save her brother and her own honor, but may also do some good for Mariana.

The reader may wonder why the Duke does not solve the dilemma by simply reassuming his control of the government. However, in doing so, he would end the play and its potential as a vehicle for a dramatic contrasting of strict law with mercy.

ACT III, SCENE ii

Summary

The Duke finds Pompey being led off to prison by the constable, Elbow. Ascertaining that he is a bawd, the Duke in his friar's guise lectures Pompey. When Lucio arrives on the scene, Pompey appeals to him to take his part, but that gentleman merely condemns him further, refusing even to go bail for him. Elbow leads Pompey away, and Lucio launches into an attack on the Duke's own virtue. The Duke challenges him to repeat his remarks to the Duke's face when he has returned. Lucio leaves, uttering still more damning remarks. Escalus now comes on the scene with Mistress Overdone in custody. Convinced that Lucio has informed against her, she charges him with getting a bawd with child and failing on his promise to marry her. In discussion with Escalus after she has departed, the Duke claims to be a friar of another country, come to Vienna on special church business. He questions Escalus about the Duke and hears his praises. Having discussed Claudio's state of mind on the eve of his execution, Escalus exits and the Duke delivers a soliloquy on the subject of false virtue.

Commentary

The minor characters of the play share a fate parallel to Claudio's in this scene. Perhaps more vulgar, but certainly no less human than that gentleman, they are deprived of their livelihood and imprisoned by the severe application of the law.

The Duke plays his friar's role again by lecturing Pompey on his vices, discoursing on the sins of the world, and telling Escalus of his progress in dealing with the condemned Claudio's fears. The disguise proves profitable to him. He is able to see how the laws are being enforced in his absence with the arrests of Pompey and Mistress Overdone. Furthermore, he can judge the loyalties of his subjects. Lucio gives himself away for an irreverent gossip in his bawdy accusations against the Duke. He insists that he would hold to his words in the presence of the Duke. Ironically, the Duke himself is his audience. Questioning Escalus, the Duke receives a good report of himself and one which proves its speaker's honesty, loyalty, and good sense. Escalus's words can be taken as a further characterization of the Duke, since he is one of his closest advisors. The Duke, he says, is a man who "above all other strifes, contended especially to know himself" (III.ii.246-47), and who took his joy from the happiness of others. The Duke, then, is an analytical man who attempts to know himself completely. He is, perhaps, just the sort of man who would disguise himself in order to check the seeming virtue of Angelo. Lucio's estimation of the Duke carries no weight, since he does not have the acquaintance with him that he claims and, in fact, as is clear in this scene, enjoys a good joke at another's expense.

Lucio refers twice in this scene to a common theme: the universality of the crime for which Claudio is condemned. The vice, he says, "is of a great kindred, it is well allied: but it is impossible to extirp it quite, friar, till eating and drinking be put down" (III. ii.108-11). Angelo's strict enforcement of the law will, according to Lucio, "unpeople the province with continency" (III.ii.184-85).

Lucio enjoys some amusement at Angelo's expense, claiming that a man so cold and so harsh against sexual crimes could not have been conceived and born in the usual fashion. His remarks to Pompey tend to condemn him rather than aid him, as Pompey had hoped. Lucio is revealed to be a man who enjoys a few witty remarks at the expense of a friend before he lifts a finger to assist him. He has even informed against Mistress Overdone. She, however, retaliates by providing the Duke with the information which he will use against Lucio in the final scene. He has gotten a whore with child and failed to keep his promise of marriage. While enjoying the plight of those around him, he is headed toward his own downfall. He is amusing, but certainly no friend. Only his actions on Claudio's behalf speak in his favor.

In his last words to Escalus, the Duke foreshadows events to come when he comments on Angelo's severity: "If his own life answer the straitness of his proceeding, it shall become him well; wherein if he chance to fail, he hath sentenced himself" (III.ii.269-71). This obvious reference to Angelo's assault upon Isabella is topped off with an entirely unnecessary soliloquy of rhymed couplets on the subject of false virtue. It is commonly speculated that this rather trite speech, jarringly out of step with the rest of the scene, was appended to it by some hand other than Shakespeare's.

The Duke promises that "disguise shall, by the disguised,/ Pay with falsehood false exacting" (III.ii.294-95). In other words, the Duke will punish Angelo's deceit with deceit of his own. The deputy's lust, disguised by counterfeit virtue, and his false promise to save Claudio's life are paid back with the Duke's own tricks: the substitute bed partner and Ragozine's head for Claudio's. Angelo gets measure for measure.

ACT IV, SCENE i

Summary

Upon his entry, the Duke finds Mariana at her home at Saint Luke's, listening to a boy singing a love ballad. Isabella soon arrives, and Mariana leaves the two to discuss their plans. She returns to meet Isabella, and then goes aside with her while Isabella outlines the Duke's idea of a substitute bed partner. Mariana agrees to the plan upon the Duke's assurances of its propriety.

Commentary

The love song with which the scene opens is much admired as one of Shakespeare's greatest. Mariana, however, is somewhat embarrassed to be found listening to music, and explains to the Duke that it appeals to her grief rather than her gaiety. One of the inconsistencies of the play is the apparent familiarity of Mariana and the disguised Duke. Although he has only been masquerading for a few days as a friar, she addresses him as though he had been her spiritual counselor for some time. Sending away the boy who has been singing for her, she says, "Here comes a man of comfort, whose advice/ Hath often still'd my brawling discontent" (IV.i.8-9). When the Duke asks Mariana to allow him a private discussion with Isabella, she replies, "I am always bound to you" (IV.i.25), as though speaking to an old friend. And again, when the Duke tells her he respects her, she answers that she knows it and has found it to be true, suggesting a long-term relationship. The reader is left to speculate that the play was rewritten hastily with resulting inconsistencies.

Another indication of some confusion of the original is the Duke's brief soliloquy, spoken while Isabella is persuading Mariana to lend herself to the scheme for Angelo's deceit. While the Duke speaks only six lines, Isabella convinces a young woman whom she has just met to have sexual relations under bizarre circumstances with a man who has spurned her. The plan is a strange one, yet the woman gives her consent in a period so short that it would hardly be possible for Isabella to relate even a sketch of the reasons behind the deceit. The Duke's lines themselves are strange, since they have no bearing upon the current scene, alluding to the deceitful gossip to which persons in great places are subject. The lines in fact seem more appropriate to the Duke's reactions in the previous scene to Lucio's falsehoods. It appears that some mix-up has occurred to confuse the scene.

In any case, Mariana agrees to the plan when the Duke sanctions it. Significantly, the Duke repeats his assurances that the scheme is not immoral or dishonorable, since Angelo is Mariana's "husband on a pre-contract" (IV.i.72).

ACT IV, SCENE ii

Summary

Given the choice of serving a prison term or becoming an executioner's assistant, Pompey chooses the latter, exiting with Abhorson to learn his new trade. The Provost informs Claudio that he is to die on the following day, along with a condemned murderer. The Duke arrives, expecting to hear of Claudio's pardon, only to be on hand as a letter is received from Angelo, urging an early morning execution. The Duke, however, persuades the Provost to spare Claudio, sending the murderer's head in his place.

Commentary

In the opening lines, where Pompey changes his trade as a bawd for the art of execution, Shakespeare comments ironically on the society in which the latter is an honorable trade. A prisoner and bawd advances himself by becoming an executioner. Abhorson regards his trade as a "mystery"; Pompey is skeptical and the Provost remarks dryly that the two "weigh equally. A feather will turn the scale" (IV.ii.31-32).

After the brief comic interlude, Claudio is called to learn of his execution the following day at eight in the morning. He accepts his fate calmly, apparently at ease with his soul. The Provost is still very much in sympathy with his case.

The Duke enters to assure himself that Angelo's end of the bargain has been carried out. The reprieve has not yet arrived, but the Duke ironically defends his deputy by telling the Provost that "his life is parallel'd/ Even with the stroke and line of his great justice . . . were he meal'd with that/ Which he corrects, then were he tyrannous" (IV.ii.82-87). The truth, of course, is that the Duke is well aware of Angelo's own shortcomings in the vice he is so determined to punish.

Angelo's crime is compounded by treachery. He writes the Provost to execute Claudio four hours earlier than his original time and to deliver the head to him. In a sense, Angelo's treachery parallels that of the Duke, Isabella, and Mariana. He is deceived by a surrogate bed partner, and he, in turn, deceives the conspirators by reneging on the promised pardon.

The Duke, however, forestalls the execution by arranging to have Barnardine, conveniently invented for the purpose, beheaded in Claudio's place. Isabella and the Duke will have the last laugh by providing a substitute head to the deputy. The Provost is at first leery of such a risky deceit, but having seen the Duke's own seal and a letter in his hand, is convinced. The Duke has arranged to make Angelo believe that he will never return to power: Angelo's tyranny is complete.

ACT IV, SCENE iii

Summary

In his new trade as executioner, Pompey finds many of his former customers housed in the prison. At Abhorson's command, he calls Barnardine to be executed, but he refuses his execution. The Duke enters and attempts to persuade Barnardine to accept his fate, but the prisoner merely reiterates his lordly refusal and returns to his cell.

Disturbed by Barnardine's unreadiness to die, the Duke is relieved when the Provost arrives with a solution. Another prisoner, similar to Claudio in coloring and age, has died of a fever. It is agreed that his head will be a substitute, and Barnardine will be hidden along with Claudio. When Isabella arrives, the disguised Duke allows her to think that her brother's execution has gone forward. He tells her that the Duke is returning and she must be present at the gates along with Angelo in order to reveal the truth and have her revenge. Lucio arrives, expressing honest grief at Claudio's death. Isabella departs, and Lucio attaches himself to the disguised Duke, slandering the absent ruler as they leave together.

Commentary

The similarity of Pompey's old trade and his new one is underlined once more when he looks about himself in the prison to discover that his clientele is very much the same. When he calls Barnardine from sleep to his execution, Pompey's manner is unchanged. He is still very much the clown: "Pray, Master Barnardine, awake till you are executed, and sleep afterwards" (IV.iii.34-35).

But Barnardine refuses his execution: "You rogue, I have been drinking all night; I am not fitted for't" (IV.iii.46-47). Shakespeare makes him a vulgar and endearing character. In prison, under sentence of death and called to his execution, he is still very much on his dignity. He refuses to put himself to the inconvenience of being executed. He treats his executioners as if they were his servants, dismissing them in a high-handed way. The critics speculate that having created Barnardine for the purpose of dying in Claudio's place, Shakespeare took such a shine to the fellow that he could not destroy him—hence the creation of yet another character, one Ragozine, already dead of a fever when we first hear of him, who provides the substitute for Claudio's head. The Duke, too, has apparently become attached to Barnardine and arranges with the Provost to have him hidden away, along with Claudio.

Setting the stage for the play's final scene, the Duke informs the Provost of his plans. He will write to Angelo, informing him of his return and desiring to be met publicly, "at the consecrated fount/ A league below the city" (IV.iii.102-3). A certain coldness enters his tone when he adds, "and from thence,/ By cold gradation and well-balanc'd form,/ We shall proceed with Angelo" (IV.iii.103-5). Though addressing the Provost, he seems almost to be speaking to himself, anticipating the ironic justice which Angelo will meet at his hands.

Critics have argued that the Duke's deceit of Isabella, in allowing her to think her brother's death has been carried out, is a cruelty which must reflect upon his character. It seems more likely that the deceit is merely a necessity of plot if the play's theme of mercy is to be carried out. Crucial to the interpretation of the last scene is Isabella's conviction that Angelo has not only used high office for his lust but that, having done his will, he has cheated on his bargain, causing her brother's execution. Through the Duke's deceit, Isabella is convinced that Angelo is not only evil, but without mercy himself. She has no reason to save her tormentor except mercy. If she were aware that her brother still lives, her mercy would be of a lesser quality, since it would demand little of her.

The jesting Lucio arrives, for once serious and genuinely saddened by Claudio's supposed death. Upon Isabella's departure, however, he reverts to his whimsical slanders of the Duke's character. And again, he delivers his witticisms ironically to the Duke himself. With double irony, Lucio comments that, "if the old fantastical duke of dark corners had been at home, he had lived" (IV.iii. 164-65). Claudio does, in fact, live, and the Duke *is* at home. Furthermore, Lucio has been most accurate in his reference to the "dark corners," since the Duke's disguise is a form of hiding. Lucio's confession that he has gotten a whore with child foreshadows the punishment which the Duke will lay down in return for his irreverence.

ACT IV, SCENE iv

Summary

Escalus and Angelo are confused by the letters they have received from the Duke, each contradictory. Now, on the verge of a return to the city, the Duke sends word that they should meet him at the gates, giving advance notice that any with grievances should be there also. Angelo considers the possibility that Isabella may take this opportunity to accuse him, but concludes that her shame and her inability to prove her claims will prevent her.

Commentary

In a soliloquy, Angelo reveals his reason for ordering Claudio's execution, contrary to his agreement with Isabella. Released, Claudio might, in time, have taken revenge. Angelo's conscience is bothering him. He regrets that Claudio is dead. His violation of Isabella amazes him. The fear that she may expose him drives him to consider the odds, and while he reasons that he is safe from her, he is still uneasy: "Alack, when once our grace we have forgot,/ Nothing goes right: we would, and we would not" (IV.iv.36-37).

ACT IV, SCENE v

Summary

Giving some letters to Friar Peter, the Duke asks him to deliver them and to call Flavius, Valentinus, Rowland, and Crassus to him. Varrius arrives as the friar is going off on his mission. The Duke greets him, tells him other friends are expected, and the two walk off together.

Commentary

Here is strong evidence that the play is not intact. The friends whom the Duke sends for here do not appear anywhere in the play, and Varrius, though he is listed in the actors of the final scene, does not speak. The purpose of the letters the Duke refers to is not clarified here or elsewhere. Plainly some confusion occurred in the publication of this play, with sections omitted, or perhaps two versions mistakenly put together. The scene does nothing by way of advancing the action or portraying the characters of the play as we have it.

ACT IV, SCENE vi

Summary

Isabella describes to Mariana what the Duke expects of them in the coming scene at the gates, and Friar Peter leads them away to accuse Angelo.

Commentary

The Duke, it appears, has advised Isabella to accuse Angelo as if she herself had yielded to his demands. Further, he has told her that he may at first appear to speak against her, but all will be right at the outcome. Friar Peter urges them to take their places at the gates.

The Duke's plans for the next scene are revealed to the audience to the extent that there will be no question of the Duke's loyalty to Isabella. The scene arouses the audience's curiosity, implying that there are yet unexpected events to come, and acts as an introduction to the final scene, building the audience's expectation toward the imminent confrontation.

ACT V, SCENE i

Summary

In a confrontation at the gates of the city, the Duke reveals the truth and administers merciful justice to all.

Isabella accuses Angelo, but Mariana comes forward to claim that she was with him herself. The Duke charges the two, along with Friar Peter, with being persuaded to their accusations by the absent Friar Lodowick (the Duke). He leaves their case to Escalus and Angelo, exiting to return shortly, disguised again as a friar. Lucio accuses him of slanders against the Duke and is helping to lead him off to prison when his hood comes off revealing the Duke.

The Duke then deals quickly with the cases at hand. He orders Angelo married at once to Mariana and then sentences him to death. Isabella pleads on his behalf, but the Duke seems impervious. He has the Provost bring out Claudio (his face covered) and Barnardine. The latter is pardoned, and when the former is revealed, the Duke pardons both Angelo and Claudio. Threatening Lucio with whipping and hanging, the Duke lets him off with marriage to the whore he has got with child. He promises a higher office to the Provost for his services, and tops off the scene by asking for Isabella's hand in marriage.

Commentary

This last scene is a lengthy one which might have been substantially shorter, had the Duke gone directly to the matter, simply explaining his disguise, the crimes he has witnessed, and going about the administration of justice. The scene, however, would have been less effective. As it is, Shakespeare builds suspense by leaving the characters of the play and its audience in doubt as to the outcome. He emphasizes his presentation of Christian mercy by having Isabella plead for Angelo while still under the impression that he has executed her brother. And he creates a mildly comic scene to finish a play which might have ended in tragedy and which would certainly have had a rather flat finale if the Duke had simply narrated his part and doled out his punishments.

A comic undertone is provided by the audience's knowledge of the Duke's identity. In his disguise, he alludes to it ironically: "The duke/ Dare no more stretch this finger of mine than he/ Dare rack his own" (V.i.315-17). Later, he protests to loving the Duke as he loves himself. Lucio's accusations against the Friar-Duke made to the Duke himself provide further comedy for the audience which knows what the actor does not. When Claudio is revealed to be still alive, the Duke's speech to Isabella has a gentle and sympathetic humor which any audience would surely warm to: "If he be like your brother, for his sake/ Is he pardon'd" (V.i.495-96).

In this final scene, the theme of merciful justice comes to the fore. The Duke seems ready to deal harshly with Isabella, Mariana, Friar Peter, and Friar Lodowick, and to apply the letter of the law in the cases of Lucio and Angelo. The mercy which he finally shows to all contrasts sharply with the rough hand of the law which he at first threatens.

" 'An Angelo for Claudio, death for death!' " he cries, "Haste still pays haste, and leisure answers leisure;/ Like doth quit like, and *Measure* still *for Measure*" (V.i.414-16). Some critics have found fault with the Duke and Shakespeare for letting Angelo off with little more than a warning for his heinous crime. Critics who interpret Angelo as a thoroughly evil man (not a fallen man of virtue) find his marriage to Mariana repellent. But in fact, there is a certain ironical justice in the conclusion of his case. His crime is, after all, one of intent only; his intention was the rape of Isabella, but instead he went to bed with a substitute. For punishment he receives the Duke's intent of execution, and only marriage with the substitute, in fact. An intended crime meets with an intended punishment, or measure for measure.

The Duke, once revealed, tells Isabella that he could not prevent her brother's death because of the short time involved, thus reiterating his claim that her brother is dead. While she might otherwise have assumed that the Duke had spared him, she still believes, when Mariana asks her to plead for Angelo, that he has been the instrument of her brother's execution. She remains silent through two lengthy pleas from Mariana, apparently struggling with her conscience, but finally makes her decision and pleads eloquently for Angelo's life. She does the Christian thing which she earlier asked Angelo to do on behalf of her brother: judge not, that ye be not judged. She has said (II.ii.67-70) that if their positions were exchanged – if he were the supplicant and she the judge – she would show him mercy, and here she proves true to her word. In another earlier scene (II.i.29-31), Angelo stated that, guilty of Claudio's crime, he would ask for the just penalty of the law, and he too lives up to his claim. "No longer session hold upon my shame,/ But let my trial be mine own confession:/ Immediate sentence then and sequent death/ Is all the grace I beg" (V.i.376-79). And again "I crave death more willingly than mercy;/ 'Tis my deserving, and I do entreat it" (V.i.481-82).

Ironically, earlier in this scene, the Duke has seemed to disbelieve Isabella's charges against Angelo, commenting, "If he had so offended,/ He would have weigh'd thy brother by himself/ And not have cut him off" (V.i.110-12). While he did not judge Claudio by himself, Angelo now asks the Duke to judge himself by Claudio's fate.

The sincerity of Angelo's repentance has been called into question, but seems true enough in the light of the evidence. The man does, in fact, ask, not once but twice, for the full measure of the law. Isabella herself, in asking mercy for the man, is moved to say, "I partly think/ A due sincerity govern'd his deeds,/ Till he did look on me" (V.i.450-52). His victim is willing to believe that his act was no more than a temporary fall from virtue. She even echoes his own words in an earlier scene (II.i.17-18) in pointing out that his crime was one of intent only: "Thoughts are no subjects;/ Intents but merely thoughts" (V.i.458-59).

In any case, a pairing off of characters in the final scene was a convention of the time. Likewise, the marriage of a wronged maiden to a repented villain was a customary ending for an Elizabethan drama. The marriages of Mariana to Angelo, Juliet to Claudio, and – with a quirk – the marriage of Lucio to his whore offer a socially acceptable solution and one which Shakespeare's audience would have viewed with approval.

The Duke has been attacked for the purportedly vicious justice he metes out to Lucio for the latter's slanders against him. The man who has excused crimes of the magnitude of Angelo's deals harshly with Lucio for his assault on the Duke's vanity. A careful reading, however, will answer these charges (V.i.524-26). As with Angelo, the Duke only pretends to sentence Lucio to whipping and hanging. From these he is excused, with marriage to a whore as his only punishment. For slanders against the Duke, he is pardoned; only the crime against his whore is punished. Lucio is, in fact, let off rather easier than the rest, since in the other cases, a measure of repentance is met with a measure of pardon, while Lucio receives his pardon without the return of repentance.

Even in this last scene, Lucio is still up to his old trick of shifting allegiances to play off one person against another, taking his humor from the dilemmas of those around him. Isabella herself is made an object of his malicious gossip, when he contributes to the case against her by reporting to have seen her with "a saucy friar,/ A very scurvy fellow" (V.i.135-36).

Isabella's detractors scorn her for marrying the Duke after making so much of her Christian commitment earlier, but the fact is that the author has made it clear that Isabella has not yet taken vows. She is, in fact, as well as in conscience, still free to marry. Further, she does not give the Duke an answer to his proposal, so the final resolution is left to the audience.

CHARACTER ANALYSES

ISABELLA

A novice, sister to Claudio. When she first appears, Isabella is about to enter the order of Saint Clare. Shakespeare portrays her as very pure and strictly moral. The audience first hears of her from her brother, who tells Lucio that she has "a prone and speechless dialect,/ Such as move men; beside, she hath prosperous art/ When she will play with reason and discourse,/ And well she can persuade" (I.ii.188-91). When Lucio asks her to turn this persuasion to her brother's good, he says to her:

> I hold you as a thing ensky'd and sainted,
> By your renouncement an immortal spirit,
> And to be talk'd with in sincerity,
> As with a saint.
>
> (I.iv.34-37)

The Duke, after knowing her briefly, regards her highly enough to offer her marriage.

Critics have held diabolically opposed views of Isabella's character. One faction sees her as one of Shakespeare's strongest and best female characters, a woman of great virtue and magnificent purity. They point to her brilliant speeches with Angelo on Christianity, power, and mercy, and to her fiery denunciation of Angelo's treachery and her brother's cowardice. She is seen as the symbol of goodness and mercy set against a background of moral decay.

The other faction sees her as self-righteous and hypocritical. They point out that she seems little concerned by her brother's crime, but is too horrified of committing the same transgression herself—even to save her brother's life. She apparently suffers no qualms, however, in asking Mariana to share Angelo's bed.

The reason for which she has been most strongly criticized is her seeming lack of sympathy for Claudio when he pleads with her to save him by giving in to Angelo's desire. She turns upon him violently, revolted by his weakness. After a scathing speech in which she tells Claudio that he is no true son of their father, she leaves him in a rage, never to speak to him again in the play.

Isabella's supporters point out that looks and actions can speak as loudly as words, and the way in which brother and sister act in the last scene might substantially soften the earlier friction between them. They further point out that the kind of deep Christian conviction and commitment that Isabella had, in combination with a sincere fondness for her brother, would cause her no little anguish when met with Angelo's demands. Certainly she was under great emotional strain during the prison scene with her brother. Perhaps the wrath which she shows him is merely her way of bolstering herself to place religious convictions above love for her brother. Her genuine affection for Claudio might also explain her failure to react with horror upon learning of his crime. In going, first, to Angelo to beg mercy for Claudio, she expresses her conflicting feelings of disgust for the crime and love for the man:

> There is a vice that most I do abhor,
> And most desire should meet the blow of justice;
> For which I would not plead, but that I must;
> For which I must not plead, but that I am
> At war 'twixt will and will not.
>
> (II.ii.29-33)

For a discussion of the factors involved in Isabella's willingness to allow Mariana to take her place in Angelo's bed, read the section entitled "The Substitute Bed Partner."

ANGELO

Deputy to the Duke. Angelo is subject to two main interpretations. He can be viewed as a thoroughly evil man, hypocritical in his pose of morality, whose lust for Isabella is true to character; or he can be seen as a basically moral man who succumbs to temptation upon one occasion.

In support of the first view, critics point out his treacherous and heartless desertion of Mariana, prior to the action of this play, showing a history of immorality. The Duke, suspecting the corruption beneath Angelo's facade of righteousness, leaves him in charge to test his true character. Angelo proceeds to convict Claudio of a most human crime. He is deaf to Isabella's pleas for mercy, but promises to save her brother if she will have sexual intercourse with him. Believing that Isabella has shared his bed, Angelo compounds his crime and cruelty by ordering Claudio's execution.

It can be argued, however, that the Duke leaves Angelo in charge because of a genuine regard for his judgement and virtue. Angelo tries to resist the temptation Isabella presents, seeking aid through prayer (in which his detractors see no sincerity). His final repentance is seen by some as evidence of his basic goodness and by others as an insincere token apology.

Perhaps a true reading of Angelo's character lies somewhere in between. Sincere in his adherence to the letter of the law, he neglects mercy. His tightly contained lower instincts burst forth with a vengeance when too strong a temptation is thrown in his path. Horrified at his own crime, he orders Claudio's execution to save himself, confident that Claudio is, after all, guilty. When the truth is discovered, he is relieved to end the deception and begs that justice without mercy be his punishment.

It is well to remember here that Shakespeare's Angelo is milder than the deputies of the sources. If Shakespeare intended to present a completely evil man, why did he not have Angelo send Claudio's head to Isabella as his counterparts did?

THE DUKE

Vincentio, Duke of Vienna. He leaves Vienna in Angelo's charge and returns disguised as Friar Lodowick to watch developments while incognito. Of some 2,600 lines in *Measure for Measure*, the Duke speaks nearly 800, only slightly less than one-third. He acts as a *deus ex machina* to turn the play from tragedy to comedy. In his omnipresence, he has been compared to a puppeteer or divinity. The godlike disguised ruler was conventional to contemporary drama. Although he controls the other characters and their actions, the Duke himself is very shallow of characterization. His purpose in leaving Vienna to his deputy and returning in disguise is unclear. He explains his motive to Friar Thomas as a wish to see long-ignored laws of morality enforced, without himself appearing as a tyrant. This implies a fatal weakness in him belied by his vigorous manipulations of the entire cast throughout the rest of the play, culminating in a dramatic confrontation of his own contriving. Angelo's critics suggest that the Duke, sensing his hypocrisy, left him in charge to test him. Possibly he saw his deputy-and-disguise method as capable of making a dramatic issue of the moral decay of Vienna and the need for law and order, while at the same time emphasizing mercy and humanity. Finally, however, it must be confessed as possible, if not actually probable, that the Duke had no logical, consistent reason for his action; perhaps he himself was a puppet of Shakespeare, who needed a device which would allow Isabella to give in to Angelo and yet maintain her virtue. The Duke is manipulated by Shakespeare into a position whence he can manipulate the other characters.

LUCIO

A gentleman of birth who keeps company with pimps, bawds, and whores. Lucio is a flip, light-minded young man, more interested in tossing off a quip than in justice, friendship, or honesty. Although he comes to Claudio's assistance by making his difficulties known to Isabella, he seems to enjoy his role as cheerleader when she makes her plea to Angelo. He blithely gives evidence against Pompey and even testifies against Isabella in the final scene. An almost conscienceless joker, he provides the audience with much humor in the form of slanders against the Duke, which he unwittingly addresses to the Duke himself. Lucio's familiarity with the characters of the underworld and society alike makes him an effective link, tying the plot and subplot together.

ESCALUS

An aged and trusted advisor to the Duke, left second in command when the Duke goes into disguise. Escalus's chief role is to act as a foil to Angelo, arguing mercy against Angelo's determination for strict enforcement of the law.

CLAUDIO

A young gentleman who has gotten Juliet with child, for which crime he is sentenced to death. He appears prominently only in Act III, Scene i, when he speaks eloquently about his fear of death. Although he is the cause of the play's action, he himself is not fully characterized. He comes to life in this scene as an intelligent and sensitive young man, only to be almost invisible throughout the remainder of the play.

PROVOST

A very human character, keeper of the prison where Claudio is held. Sympathy for Claudio's case prompts him to risk his position and even his life to plead with Angelo for mercy, and finally, to prevent Claudio's execution.

POMPEY

Mistress Overdone's pimp, he exchanges his profession for that of executioner in order to avoid a jail term. The clown of the play, he takes life in stride and with humor.

MISTRESS OVERDONE

Keeper of a whorehouse who loses her livelihood when Angelo cracks down on moral offenders.

BARNARDINE

A prisoner created by the author to die in Claudio's place. Shakespeare found him too likeable to destroy and had the Duke give this haughty, drunken swaggerer a pardon.

MARIANA

Betrothed of Angelo. She acts as substitute bed partner to him for Isabella. A device of plot, she is not characterized.

JULIET

Promised to Claudio, though not formally betrothed, she expects his child. Juliet speaks only a few lines in one scene, although she is on stage in two others. Like Mariana, she is a device of plot and is given no characterization.

CRITICAL INTERPRETATION AND TEXTUAL ANALYSES

Measure for Measure is one of Shakespeare's most controversial works. Scholars and critics have long held widely differing views on the play's quality and interpretation of its three major characters: Angelo, Isabella, and the Duke. The play has been highly praised as excellent comedy and roundly criticized as tragedy badly adapted to romantic comedy. It has been called unsatisfactory and inconsistent on the one hand, and defended as effective, realistic, and bold in its characterizations on the other.

Coleridge proclaimed it a "painful play" made of "disgusting" comedy and "horrible" tragedy. Hardin Craig has called it "one of

Shakespeare's worst plays." Mark Van Doren, in defense of the poet, claims that the play contains "some of his gravest, most complex, and most effective poetry." On this point, at least, the critics are in substantial agreement, noting a handful of key speeches written in Shakespeare's finest style. Masefield calls *Measure for Measure* "one of the greatest works of the greatest English mind."

Although the play's characterizations have been praised, it is here that the critics are in greatest conflict. Attacks upon all three of the main characters have a violence seldom found in literary criticism. Each of the characters has adherents who defend and praise with as much energy and emotion as the attackers show in opposition. The intent of this commentary, however, is to provide the reader with sound interpretation, taking the play at its face value. Alternate interpretations are also mentioned. It is left to the individual to discover the reading most satisfactory to him personally.

FORM

Although included in the Comedy section of the First Folio, *Measure for Measure* has been called tragedy, tragicomedy, satire, and allegory by its critics. Scholars have argued that the play is a comedy only by the force of the contrived happy ending. Its theme, characters, and action are tragic, and only the manipulations of the Duke, who acts as a *deus ex machina*, bring the play to a happy conclusion. The eloquent poetic passages on the ephemerality of life and the fear of death's unknown realm are cited as indications of the tragic style.

The play has been related to Shakespeare's personal life. The poet is said to have been immersed in a tragic vein at the time *Measure for Measure* was written. He was in the midst of the creative flow which produced his great tragedies: *Hamlet, Othello, King Lear,* and *Macbeth.* A "sex nausea" is said to have overcome him at this period. Scholars have seen the evidence of collaboration in the play as implication that Shakespeare's devotion to the play was half-hearted, that he had no stomach for comedy at this time of his life. Biographical evidence is slight, however, and theories are based mainly upon the content of the plays and sonnets. It is only speculation to assume that the play suffered from its author's depression, sex revulsion, or tragic mood.

In considering what genre the play exemplifies, it is well to note that comedy in Shakespeare's time was chiefly identified by its happy ending. Conventions of romantic comedy of the seventeenth century included an idealized heroine, love as the basic theme, and a problem brought to happy conclusion. Tragicomedy offered a tragic theme with a happy close brought about by the intervention of a *deus ex machina.* Conventions included characters of noble rank, love as the central theme (its ideal forms contrasted with the vulgar), disguise, and virtue and vice thrown into sharp contrast. Clearly, *Measure for Measure* might fall into either category and may reasonably be considered both romantic comedy and tragicomedy. Thrall's *Handbook to Literature** notes that tragicomedy was developed by Beaumont and Fletcher around 1610, some six years after Shakespeare penned *Measure for Measure.* Although *Measure for Measure* is one of its type, the form was not defined until later.

Numerous modern critics have objected to the abrupt appearance of a happy ending, but the reader should keep in mind that this was a convention of romantic comedy with which Shakespeare's audience was well acquainted.

SUBPLOT

The characters and action of the subplot parallel to some extent those of the plot. Pompey and Mistress Overdone suffer from the sudden enforcement of Vienna's morality laws, as does Claudio. Elbow, the simple-minded constable, enforces the laws in the subplot as Angelo does in the main plot. The subplot, however, is not developed to the extent that it might stand alone, as is frequently the case in Shakespeare's plays. The low characters provide more of an undercurrent than a minor plot. Their chief role is to provide comic relief from the tragedy which pervades the plot. For while the play is a comedy, much of its action is of a tragic nature.

---

*William Flint Thrall and Addison Hibbard, *A Handbook to Literature,* rev. and enl. by C. Hugh Holman (New York: The Odyssey Press, 1960), pp. 534-35.

The minor characters are earthy, lively, and amusing. Although some critics see them as vulgar and obscene representatives of a society rotten with moral corruption, the humor they invoke and the sympathy they command lend weight to the argument that their creator is pleased with them. A director might manipulate his actors to make the low characters either funny or disgusting, but the harmlessness of their wit seems to indicate that Shakespeare meant them to be amusing.

THE SUBSTITUTE BED PARTNER

Mariana's substitution for Isabella in Angelo's bed (sometimes called the bed trick) has received considerable attention from scholars. Isabella has been sharply criticized for her willingness to allow Mariana to make such a sacrifice. The heroine's purity has been challenged on the basis of her easy compliance with the Duke's scheme, which calls for Mariana to commit the very sin which so repulses Isabella. The Duke's character has been maligned for the perpetration of this vulgar trick. He is, critics charge, as immoral as the play's corrupt setting. Even the gentle Mariana has been attacked for her role in the deception.

Before making a judgement on the characters or their creator, however, it is important to gain an understanding of the conventions operating on Shakespeare's contemporary audience. When the play was written in 1604, it was customary to have a formal ceremony of betrothal some time before the actual wedding celebration. The betrothal involved repetition of vows and gave conjugal rights to the betrothed. By this custom, it was no more immoral for Angelo and Mariana to share a bed than if they had actually been married.

Claudio and Juliet's secret betrothal, on the other hand, did not carry with it the conjugal rights, since it was simply an exchange of promises, not formally witnessed or celebrated. For this reason, Claudio and Juliet are guilty of a crime and immorality, while Mariana's union with Angelo carries with it no stigma.

An awareness of the custom of betrothal casts a new light on the play. Not only does it clear the Duke, Isabella, and Mariana of impurity, but it also has the effect of lessening Claudio's crime, since there is only a question of a formal public betrothal between crime and convention.

The bed trick is admittedly a contrived bit of dramatic foolery, requiring an audience to believe that a woman can, without discovery, go to bed with a man who knows her and expects another. It further requires that an audience credit the woman's willingness to take part in such a deception after being heartlessly cast off by the man years previously. And finally, the existence of a Mariana who can be Isabella's proxy without smirching her own character is itself an unlikely bit of coincidence.

However, coincidence and the failure of a man to recognize his lover were established conventions of Renaissance drama. The deserted wife's return in disguise to her husband was traditional. Shakespeare's audiences were accustomed to accepting in the theater what they would have scoffed at in real life. The modern reader, then, should bear in mind that the bed trick would not have seemed as extraordinary to Shakespeare's original audience as it does to him.

Although contrived, it is certainly necessary. In order to bring the play to its final dramatic conclusion, while maintaining Isabella's virtue, Shakespeare had to devise a way to allow her to refuse Angelo's demands while making him think they had been met. Actual compliance would have stained Isabella's purity, damaging her as a symbol of good and destroying the dramatic effect of virtue set against corruption. A flat refusal would have meant that Claudio's execution would go forward unhindered, bringing the play to a conclusion with no opportunity for repentance, forgiveness, and the application of justice with mercy which together form the play's theme.

TITLE

The title of *Measure for Measure* is taken from the Bible: "Judge not, that you be not judged. For with the judgement you pronounce you will be judged and the measure you give will be the measure you get" (Matthew 7.1 and 7.2). This quotation from Christ's Sermon on the Mount, stating generally that each individual will be judged as harshly as he has judged others, implies that mercy and human sympathy should temper justice.

In Mark, the thought is expressed again: "And he said to them, 'Take heed what you hear; the measure you give will be the measure you get, and still more will be given you' " (Mark 4.24).

It is interesting to note that the phrase also appears in one of Shakespeare's earlier plays, *The Third Part of King Henry VI:* "Measure for measure must be answered" (II.vi.55).

THEME

The theme of *Measure for Measure* is the temperance of justice with mercy. Merciful justice is juxtaposed throughout with strict enforcement of the law. The Duke, Isabella, Escalus, Mariana, and the Provost all advocate mercy. Only Angelo demands strict adherence to the law, even to recommending his own execution when his deeds are discovered.

Treated with mercy, the play's criminals respond with repentance, making forgiveness and repentance another theme. Also considered thematic is the question of hypocrisy versus true virtue. *Measure for Measure* has been called satirical of hypocritical, self-righteous Puritanism. The playwright must certainly have been aware of Puritanism, a religious movement on the rise in his time, since Puritans loudly denounced the theater as immoral.

RELATIONSHIP TO SHAKESPEARE'S OTHER PLAYS

Measure for Measure was written during the same period as Shakespeare's great tragedies: 1601 to 1608. In this brief time span, he wrote *Hamlet, Othello, King Lear,* and *Macbeth,* as well as *Julius Caesar, Timon of Athens, Coriolanus,* and *Antony and Cleopatra.* Critics frequently point out that *Measure for Measure* could easily have been a tragedy itself. The plot, the characters, and the setting are all potentially tragic. The happy ending is so sudden as to seem contrived, leaving critics to speculate that the play was meant for a tragedy and was turned to comedy at the last moment. Perhaps the poet was so immersed in his tragic masterpieces that their mood was reflected in this work. Or he may have experienced dark and bitter times in his personal life at this period. Audience demands may have influenced him to make comedy of tragic material. Pulled away from his major works to write it, he gave it less than his best. While these variously advanced ideas are no more than speculation, many critics do agree that the play has no consistency of mood, the subject matter is more tragic than comic, and the final scene is jarring.

Measure for Measure is often treated with *All's Well that Ends Well* and *Troilus and Cressida*. Written during the great tragic period, they are often called "bitter" or "dark comedies." They are also known as the "problem comedies" because they examine a grave problem of human existence in a style which is more serious than usual for comedy, yet not strictly tragic either. The play is preceded by Shakespeare's great comedies and is followed by the romances.

All's Well that Ends Well, written about 1598, or six years previous to *Measure for Measure*, turns on the same dramatic device, the substitution of one bed partner for another. Critics point out that while this works well as a part of the plot in *All's Well*, in *Measure for Measure* it seems tacked on. In need of a convenient way to prevent the necessity of Isabella's giving way to Angelo's lewd demands, the author recalled the bed trick from his earlier work and simply inserted it.

Like *Measure for Measure*, *Othello* found its source in Cinthio's *Hecatommithi*. Written in the same year, it was introduced at court in November, 1604, a few weeks before *Measure for Measure*.

The play also bears a noticeable resemblance to *Hamlet* in two of its passages. Angelo's speech on prayers is often compared to that of King Claudius in *Hamlet*. The inability of a conscience heavy with guilt to give sincerity to prayer is expressed by Angelo in Act II, Scene iv, line 1 ff.:

When I would pray and think, I think and pray
To several subjects. Heaven hath my empty words;
Whilst my invention, hearing not my tongue,
Anchors on Isabel: Heaven in my mouth,
As if I did but only chew his name;
And in my heart the strong and swelling evil
Of my conception.

Angelo's words clearly recall King Claudius's struggle to pray in Act III, Scene iii, lines 97-98 of *Hamlet:*

My words fly up, my thoughts remain below.
Words without thoughts never to heaven go.

Claudio expresses his fears of the unknown in death to his sister Isabella in a speech which clearly echoes Hamlet's famous soliloquy in III.i.56-88 ("To be, or not to be . . . "):

> Ay, but to die, and go we know not where;
> To lie in cold obstruction and to rot;
> This sensible warm motion to become
> A kneaded clod; and the delighted spirit
> To bathe in fiery floods, or to reside
> In thrilling region of thick-ribbed ice;
> To be imprison'd in the viewless winds,
> And blown with restless violence round about
> The pendent world; or to be worse than worst
> Of those that lawless and incertain thought
> Imagine howling: 'tis too horrible!
> The weariest and most loathed wordly life
> That age, ache, penury and imprisonment
> Can lay on nature is a paradise
> To what we fear of death.
>
> (III.i.116-32)

SELECTED BIBLIOGRAPHY

Brandes, Georg. *William Shakespeare.* New York: Macmillan Company, 1924, pp. 401-10.
Treats *Measure for Measure* as an attack on Puritan hypocrisy.

Burton, Philip. *The Sole Voice; Character Portraits from Shakespeare.* New York: Dial Press, 1970, pp. 201-16.
Character study of Angelo, with minor treatment of Isabella.

Campbell, Oscar James. "Shakespeare's Union of Comedy and Satire." in *His Infinite Variety; Major Shakespearean Criticism since Johnson.* Edited by Paul N. Siegel. Philadelphia: J.B. Lippincott Company, 1964, pp. 154-92.
Considers *Measure for Measure* as a satire.

Chambers, E. K. *William Shakespeare; A Study of Facts and Problems.* London: Oxford University Press, 1930, vol. I, pp. 452-57.
Discusses the problem of how much of the play is Shakespeare's own and what portions have been revised.

Chambers, R. W. "Measure for Measure," in *His Infinite Variety; Major Shakespearean Criticism since Johnson.* Edited by Paul

N. Siegel. Philadelphia: J.B. Lippincott Company, 1964, pp. 162-92.
Development of the idea that *Measure for Measure* is a deeply Christian play based on forgiveness and taking its theme and title from the Sermon on the Mount.

Charlton, H. B. *Shakespearian Comedy,* 4th ed. London: Methuen and Company, 1938, pp. 208-65.
Sees the play as humane, not cynical, asserting that the author's dark comedies were of an earlier period. Treats all three of the so-called Problem Plays. Especially pages 212-16 and 248-58.

Craig, Hardin. *An Interpretation of Shakespeare.* New York: Dryden Press, 1948, pp. 220-22, 228-36.
General summary, background, and criticism with frequent references to variant interpretations of the play.

Lawrence, William Witherle. *Shakespeare's Problem Comedies.* New York: Macmillan Company, 1931, pp. 1-9 and 78-121.
General analysis of the play in terms of contemporary conventions and its construction from the sources.

Leech, Clifford. "The 'meaning' of *Measure for Measure,*" in *Shakespeare; The Comedies; A Collection of Critical Essays.* Edited by Kenneth Muir. Englewood Cliffs, N.J.: Prentice-Hall, Inc., 1965, pp. 109-18.
Discusses the inconsistencies of theme and characterization.

Munro, John, ed. *The London Shakespeare: A New Annotated and Critical Edition of the Complete Works in Six Volumes.* New York: Simon and Schuster, 1957, vol. ii. pp. 967-74.
A conglomeration of what the critics have said of the play. Good, quick overview of divergent opinions.

Parrott, Thomas Marc. *Shakespearean Comedy.* New York: Russel and Russell, Inc., 1949, pp. 335-65.
A good general discussion of the play and its varying interpretations.

Raleigh, Walter. *Shakespeare.* London: Macmillan and Company, Ltd., 1965, pp. 164-73.
Consideration of critics' views and presentation of a mild and sympathetic interpretation. Enjoyable reading.

Rowse, A. L. *William Shakespeare; A Biography.* New York: Harper and Row, 1963, pp. 360-65.
Sees theme as justice without hypocrisy. Considers the author

to have been in sympathy with the loose morality of the setting, and involved with the play.

Van Doren, Mark. *Shakespeare*. New York: Henry Holt and Company, 1939, pp. 217-24.
— Emphasizes the moral corruption of a society as the author's theme and the dominating factor in the action.

Questions: Could Othello have conveyed one part of a scena & Measure the other?

— Is Isabella's response & hand of the situation one half of Cass and Lucrece the other? Wha can a woman decide? She is either prude or suicidally sham.

— Isabella takes Portia's Christianity one step further? She must forgive in order to sa a life (she is not God; she can decide to judge — her speech with angelo points out how he acts like God). But she know the daily death that the decisio to save her brother would bring — this is her human side.